BE THE CHANGE!

RIGHTS FOR MIGRANTS AND REFUGEES

HOW YOU CAN MAKE A DIFFERENCE

Robert Tuesley Anderson

BROWN BEAR BOOKS

Published by Brown Bear Books Ltd
4877 N. Circulo Bujia
Tucson, AZ 85718
USA

and

G14, Regent Studios
1 Thane Villas
London N7 7PH
UK

ISBN 978-1-78121-948-5 (ALB)
ISBN 978-1-78121-954-6 (paperback)

Library of Congress Cataloging-in-Publication Data available on request

Design Manager: Keith Davis
Children's Publisher: Anne O'Daly
Picture Manager: Sophie Mortimer

Picture Credits
Cover: iStock: Anwar Saichu (background); Shutterstock: New Africa. Interior: Alamy: Associated Press 27,
Guy Corbishley 26, NurPhoto SRL 18, PA Images 23; iStock: farma51 16, FG Trade 22; Public Domain: National
Library of Austria/Ferdinand Schmutzer/restored by Adam Cuerden 19; Shutterstock: Rasid Aslim 5,
BalkansCat 12-13, Ringo Chiu 7, Everett Historical 6, 8, Johan Hafiz 9, mady70 17, Bruno Mameli 20, Timo
Nausch 11, Peopleimages.com- Yuri A 10, quetios123 15, David Peinado Romero 21, Tolga Sezgin 14,
SpeedKingz 25, Ververidis Vasilis 4. United States Government: FDR Presidential Library and Museum 13

All artwork and other photography Brown Bear Books.

Brown Bear Books has made every attempt to contact the copyright holder.
If you have any information about omissions, please contact: licensing@brownbearbooks.co.uk

Manufactured in the United States of America
CPSIA compliance information: Batch#AG/5657

Websites
The website addresses in this book were valid at the time of going to press. However, it is possible
that contents or addresses may change following publication of this book. No responsibility for
any such changes can be accepted by the author or the publisher. Readers should be supervised
when they access the Internet.

Contents

Introduction

Around the world, more than 280 million people are migrants and refugees, and the number is increasing all the time. They may be fleeing violence or famine, or they may be looking for a better life and opportunities. Many migrants face danger and violence, not just on their journey, but when they arrive in a new country.

Some migrants can migrate legally. They enter another country with a passport and visa. They can apply to stay in the country and may eventually have the right to become a citizen. However, many more have to migrate illegally and in secret.

Migrating illegally puts people in danger. They may have to travel in unsafe boats, in the backs of airless lorries, or even by swimming across a river or sea. They may have paid money to unscrupulous people smugglers. When they reach a safe country, they often have few rights and face poor living conditions and an uncertain future.

A boatload of migrants and refugees reach the Greek island of Lesbos after a dangerous sea crossing in a dinghy. They are seeking safety and a better life.

Little Amal is greeted in London, England. The 12-foot (3.7-m) puppet represents a Syrian child refugee. She visits different countries to draw attention to the plight of child refugees.

Definitions

Many migrants do not freely choose to migrate. War, economic hardship, political oppression, and climate change force people to leave their country and seek a new life elsewhere. Others leave because they risk being imprisoned or killed due to their political views or religion. The United Nations uses the term "refugee" for someone who has been forced to escape war or persecution. It uses the term "migrant" for a person who is seeking a better life, but could return to their country without facing danger.

While we can do little about the conditions that force people to leave their homelands, we may be able to do a great deal to help migrants in our countries. We can stand up for migrant rights. We can persuade our governments to give treat them with respect. And we can encourage our friends and families to provide a welcoming environment. We can all be migrant activists, and this book will show you how.

Chapter 1

Understanding the Arguments

People have been migrants since the earliest times. The first humans in Africa moved around an area, gathering food or hunting animals. When populations became too big, the climate changed, or food became scarce, they moved to new areas.

Settlers and Migrants

Things changed with the development of farming, some 10,000 years ago. Many people settled in permanent communities. Over time, nations were established. People still migrated, however, looking for better land and resources.

Migrations like these could result in violence. Newcomers might displace the people already living in an area, disrupting their way of life and even driving them from their land. With time, relations between the newcomers and the settled people could become more peaceful and cooperative. Their cultures might merge, and a new blended culture develop.

Women arrive at Ellis Island, an immigration station in New York Harbor. Between 1892 and 1924, more than 12 million people passed through the center.

Migrants from Guatemala hand themselves in to the US Border Patrol. Many are driven from their homeland by the impact of the climate crisis.

Emergency Files

US–Mexican Border

Today, many migrants to the United States cross the border from Mexico. Between 2021 and 2022, the US Border Patrol encountered 1.6 million migrants trying to cross into the United States. The migrants come from Mexico but also from many other Central and South American countries. They are fleeing poverty and gang violence and seeking better job opportunities. The illegal migration routes from Mexico to the United States are among the most dangerous in the world. Hundreds of people die each year, often from heat stroke and lack of water as they try to cross inhospitable deserts.

The United States is a story of how migration helped create a country. Successive waves of migrants came to North America from Europe and other places seeking religious freedom, new opportunities, or relief from poverty. However, in doing so, they pushed many Indigenous peoples (Native Americans) from their lands into reservations, and killed many others.

Forced Migrations

The transatlantic slave trade was the largest forced migration of peoples in history. More than 12 million Africans were forcibly taken from their homes and removed to the Americas to be enslaved people. They endured brutality and loss of freedom, their culture, and family life.

Forced migration has continued into recent times. During and after World War I (1914–1918) and World War II (1939–1945), many peoples were deported from their homelands and resettled elsewhere. For example, from 1944 to 1946, the Soviet Union forced over a million Poles to leave their homes after their homelands became part of Soviet territory. During the Yugoslav Wars (1991–2001) in eastern Europe, ethnic Serbians living in Bosnia expelled up to 30,000 Bosnian Muslims.

Captured Africans were marched, usually chained or tied together, to the coast. From there, they were shipped to the Americas.

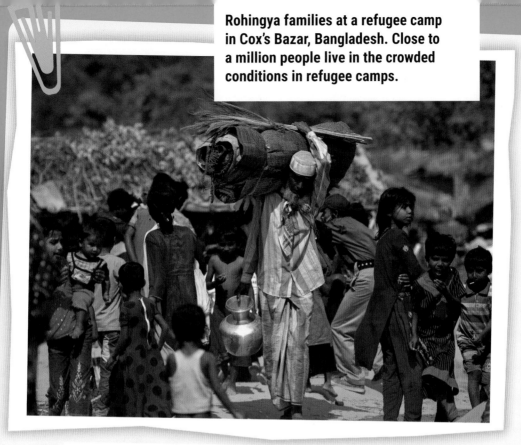

Rohingya families at a refugee camp in Cox's Bazar, Bangladesh. Close to a million people live in the crowded conditions in refugee camps.

Emergency Files

The Rohingya

Forced migration is still taking place today. The Rohingya are a Muslim people who traditionally live on the western coast of Myanmar. As Muslims in a Buddhist-majority state they have long faced discrimination and persecution. Government violence against the Rohingya increased rapidly after 2016, and an estimated million Rohingya have been forced to flee to neighboring Bangladesh. They settled in two overcrowded camps, where there is often a shortage of food and safe water and where infectious diseases are common. The Bangladeshi government has in turn relocated thousands of Rohingya refugees, a number against their will, to a remote island off its shores.

International travelers are asked to show a passport. They may also be asked questions, including the purpose of their visit and how long they will be staying.

Controlling Migration

As nations developed, governments brought in laws to control who migrates into their country. They may set quotas or limits on the number of migrants they will accept, and they may restrict migration to people who do certain jobs. They set patrols on their borders and set up checks in seaports and airports to make sure people are traveling legally.

To cross freely, people usually have to show a passport or an identity card, and sometimes a visa, too. A visa is a permission to stay for a certain period and for certain reasons, such as work or study. Migrants usually have to apply for permission to move to a country before they enter it. Some, however, may be able to claim asylum as a refugee after they arrive.

The world's poorest people often do not have passports or other documentation and so find it very difficult to enter countries legally. Yet they are often the people who need to migrate in order to escape poverty or persecution.

The Rainbow Railroad

In the news media and politics, migrants are often portrayed as a group, rather than as individuals, each with their own story to tell. But migrants are as diverse as everyone else. Some, for example, identify as LGBTQ+, and are escaping persecution and violence in their home countries. Same-sex relationships are illegal in about 70 countries, and in six countries people face the death penalty.

The Rainbow Railroad is a Canadian and US charity that works to provide emergency assistance to LGBTQ+ people and to bring them to a safe country. Since it started in 2006, the organization has helped around 10,000 people to find safety.

A protest in Germany shows support and solidarity with LQBTQ+ refugees and migrants.

Chapter 2

International Action

International organizations and governments have tried to address the issue of migration and the challenges it raises. Often, they try to balance migrants' rights with the difficulties faced by host countries. Meanwhile, campaign groups have pushed for more humane migration systems, as well as fighting for migrant rights and showing the positive contributions migrants make.

Speak Up

UNHCR

UNHCR is the United Nations' Refugee Agency. It was set up in 1950, after World War II, to help the millions of people who lost their homes as a result of the conflict. Today it works in 135 countries, providing support, including food, shelter, and medical care, for people forced to flee their homeland. In the longer term, the agency works with governments to improve laws that protect refugees.

A UNHCR worker helps people crossing the border between Serbia and Croatia.

Eleanor Roosevelt holding the Universal Declaration of Human Rights. She chaired the committee that drafted the document.

International Law

Migrant rights are protected by international laws and conventions. These have been laid down since the end of World War II (1939–1945).

The most important of these is the United Nations' International Declaration of Human Rights, which was adopted in 1948. It gives migrants the same rights as any other person, wherever they are and wherever they go. Article 14 of the declaration states that "Everyone has the right to seek and to enjoy in other countries asylum from persecution."

Honoring Rights

All 193 countries that are members of the United Nations have signed the Declaration of Human Rights, but they have different records when it comes to honoring those rights. Many countries have struggled with the rising number of refugees. They are often poorly equipped to host them, and refugees can end up living in poor and overcrowded accommodation while their claims for refugee status are processed. This can take a long time. Some political parties exploit fear of migrants and refugees to help them win power in elections.

Where Do Refugees Live?

Around 70 percent of refugees live in countries that neighbor their home country. Turkey hosts the highest number of refugees, followed by Iran and then Columbia. The cost of supporting refugees is not shared equally. According to the UNHCR, the majority of refugees are hosted in low- and middle-income countries, which struggle to provide the housing, education, and healthcare that refugees need.

This camp in Turkey was built to house Syrian families escaping the war in their country. Built for 23,000 people, it has more than 36,000 inhabitants.

A Syrian child at the border between Syria and Turkey. Many Syrian children have never known peace in their country.

Children on the Move

In 2015, a two-year-old Syrian Kurdish boy named Alan Kurdi was found drowned on a beach in Turkey. His family had been fleeing the Syrian War and trying to cross the Adriatic Sea to Greece in a small inflatable boat. Alan's death brought home the plight of many migrant children, who are especially vulnerable to the challenges of migration. Around half of the world's refugees are children. Many migrate by themselves. They can find themselves homeless and vulnerable to criminals, and can have even fewer rights than adults. For example, in the United Kingdom child migrants who come alone and gain refugee status cannot win permission for relatives to join them.

Chapter 3

It Starts with You

News stories can make us think that migrants and refugees are somewhere else—on leaky boats, in makeshift camps on borders in another country, or in overcrowded detention centers. In fact, migrants are everywhere.

Migrants may be our neighbors. They may be learning in our classrooms and working in local businesses. They may be teaching in schools and helping in hospitals. Many people reading this book will be migrants, or the children or grandchildren of migrants.

Just Like Me

We can make a big difference to migrants' rights and migrants' lives simply by starting to think of migrants as being—for all their differences—just like us. They may have a different culture, background, or religion, even different values, from us. They may be legal or illegal migrants. Whatever their background, they have just the same rights as we do.

Does your school have a buddy scheme to help migrant students settle in? Perhaps you could volunteer to be one.

The war in Ukraine drove around 5.1 million people from their country. Most settled in Europe.

Try to find out as much about the migrant groups who live in your neighborhood. For example, your community may be hosting Ukrainians who have fled the war in their home country. If so, there may be Ukrainian children in your school. You could find out more about Ukrainian traditions, food, or culture, or what is happening in their country. A Ukrainian classmate may want to talk about their country and their experiences. Perhaps they miss their home or are worried about relatives they left behind. Listen and ask questions as sensitively as you can. Express your solidarity!

An activist takes part in a demonstration on International Migrants Day, showing their solidarity with migrant workers.

Speak Up

International Migrants Day

International Migrants Day is celebrated each year on December 18. This is a day for expressing solidarity with migrants, recognizing the huge contributions they make, and promoting their rights. You can get involved by asking your school to take part in the celebration, for example, by staging an exhibition telling migrant stories or holding a rally. Be creative and get as many as your fellow students involved as you can.

Activism at School

Migrants and refugees—especially children—need to feel safe and protected, especially if they have fled war or violence or have faced poverty and famine. You can help them feel safe by helping to create a friendly, supportive, and welcoming environment within your school. A school should be a safe space for everyone, whatever their background. Your teachers have a big part in creating that space, of course, but so do you!

You could also raise awareness of the issues relating to migrants. Work with your teachers and fellow students to highlight key issues: the reasons for migration, the hardships faced by child migrants, and so on. Ask your teachers to invite migrant speakers into the school to talk about their experiences, not just their migration journey but how they adapted to living in your country. You might hold a class or school debate. You could research famous migrants and refugees and present their life stories.

Physicist Albert Einstein was a refugee from Nazi Germany. He helped found the International Relief Association to help other refugees.

Chapter 4

Stand Together

As a budding activist, the best and easiest way to become more involved in supporting migrants and refugees is through existing organizations that help migrants in various ways.

Many will have a section on their website called "Get involved." One option often on offer is to fundraise. There are lots of ways to raise money: sponsored runs, wheelchair walks, bungee jumps. You could arrange a bake sale or sell old books, games, or clothes that you no longer need.

You could get involved in campaigns or attend rallies or protests. You could approach an organization directly and ask how you can get involved. They may have the perfect idea! Your support will help send a message to governments that they need to act and change the way migrants are treated and according to international law.

Get creative! These origami paper boats were part of a protest that linked migrant justice with climate change.

The Butterfly Effect stands up for migrant children detained at the US border. Their message is "All kids should be free and with the people who love them."

Speak Up

The Butterfly Effect

The Butterfly Effect is a youth activist group in California. It started in 2019 to support young migrants who have crossed the US–Mexican border, especially those held in detention centers. The name refers to the spectacular annual migrations of Monarch butterflies but also to the idea that small actions can end up bringing about big changes. Their slogan is: "Migration is beautiful." Find out more about them at: butterflyeffectmigration.org.

Are there any local donation centers, collecting clothes and toys for refugees and migrants? Could you help them collect useful items?

Set Up a Campaign

Sometimes we can be inspired to begin our own campaigns to support migrants. You might want to help make migrants feel more welcome in your community. You might have seen migrants being treated badly or know fellow students whose family is facing deportation. We can feel angry at the injustice or lack of humanity shown by the political system and feel the need to act straight away.

Stop and think how you can best work in the interests of your migrant friend or the migrant community. Get a teacher or parent involved and ask for their advice. Possible options might be: school or community petitions; writing to politicians; or staging a peaceful rally to raise awareness. These acts may seem small, but they can have powerful consequences.

Speak Up

The Glasgow Girls

In 2005, seven school friends in Glasgow, Scotland, began a campaign to draw attention to the plight of asylum seekers. The UK Border Force had detained a friend and her family in a dawn raid. The family were Roma people from Kosovo. They had been seeking asylum but their application failed. With the help of a teacher, the seven young women organized a school petition. Eventually this gained the attention of the Scottish Parliament and government. The "Glasgow Girls," as they were known, met with the Scottish First Minister, who promised to make changes to how migrants were treated. In 2008, the Roma friend and family were finally given the right to stay in the United Kingdom.

Three of the Glasgow Girls—from left, Agnesa Murselaj, Amal Azzudin, and Roza Salih. In 2022, Roza was elected a Glasgow city councillor.

Chapter 5

Your Activist Toolkit

There are many ways to get involved as an activist for migrant and refugee rights, and there are lots of organizations and campaigns that can help.

Speak Up

Migrant and Refugee Organizations

United Nations High Commissioner for Refugees (UNHCR) (www.unhcr.org), a global organization that seeks to protect migrant lives and rights.

Refugee Council (refugeecouncil.org.uk), a UK charity that campaigns for a more humane asylum system. Other countries have similar organizations, for example the Refugee Council USA (rcusa.org), and the Canadian Council for Refugees (ccrweb.ca/en).

Young Center for Immigrant Children's Rights (www.theyoungcenter.org), an organization that works to protect the rights of unaccompanied and separated young children.

Rainbow Railroad (www.rainbowrailroad.org), an organization that helps LGBTQ+ people to escape persecution in their own country and find safety and wellbeing on a new one.

Does your school have a newsletter? Researching and writing a story, and sharing it in a school newsletter, is an effective way to raise awareness.

Volunteer

Volunteering with a migrants' rights organization is a great way to help make change. Many organizations need volunteers to help run their campaigns, by handing out leaflets or helping in their office.

You could also raise awareness of different campaigns at your school. Perhaps you could arrange a stall, with leaflets, or talk to your teachers about inviting a speaker from a campaign to visit your class? Write articles about migrant campaigns for your school newspaper or website. You might be able to interview someone who came to your school as a migrant or refugee to put across their perspective.

Taking Action

Events such as International Migrants Day are an opportunity to celebrate the contributions that migrants make to our communities. Find out if an event is happening near to where to live. If not, why not organize something at your school or in your neighborhood?

March!

Campaigns for migrant and refugee rights often organize marches and other events to highlight a particular cause or protest inhumane treatment. Large-scale events are great ways to show politicians that people care about migrants and refugees. They are also a way to meet other people who support your cause and start to build a network of activists. Working together, we can make change happen!

Whether large or small, marches and rallies are a display of strength and solidarity.

Role Models

Learning about other young people who are migrant and refugee activists can provide role models for your own campaigns. Here are some people who took a stand for migrants. Use the Internet to find out more about their stories, and to discover more inspiring activists.

Roza Salih: Kurdish-born refugee activist and one of the Glasgow Girls who campaigned against the deportation of child migrants in Scotland.

Lili Ellis and Kala Marbin: founders of the youth activist group The Butterfly Effect, which campaigns to protect and help child migrants detained at the US–Mexican border.

Sarah and Yusra Mardini: two sisters who fled Syria in 2015 and crossed the Aegean Sea with other refugees in an overcrowded dinghy. When the boat began to sink, Sarah, Yusra, and two others swam for three hours to pull the dinghy to safety on the Greek island of Lesbos. The sisters settled in Germany and are now human rights activists.

Yusra (left) and Sarah were competition swimmers in Syria. Yusra competed in the 2016 Olympic Games as part of a Refugee Olympic Team.

Timeline

1891 The Bureau of Immigration is set up in the United States

1892 Ellis Island, the United States' first immigration station, opens in New York Harbor

1917 The Immigration Act is passed in the United States; it requires immigrants aged 16 and above to demonstrate that they can read

1921 and 1924 The Emergency Quota Act of 1921 and the Immigration Act of 1924 set limits on the number of immigrants that can enter the United States from different countries

1945 By the end of the Second World War, more than 40 million people are refugees

1948 The Universal Declaration of Human Rights lays down the basic rights of all people

1950 The United Nations set up the United Nations High Commissioner for Refugees (UNHCR), also known as the UN Refugee Agency

1951 The UN Refugee Convention sets out an internationally recognized definition of a refugee

1967 The 1967 Protocol Relating to the Status of Refugees expands the UN Refugee Convention

1972 In Uganda, President Idi Amin orders the explusion of Ugandan-Asians, most of whom move to the United Kingdom

1975	The end of the Vietnam War initiates the flight of almost 2 million Vietnamese, often in unsafe, leaky boats
2006	The Secure Fence Act strengthens the building of fencing along the US–Mexican border to stop migrants crossing into the United States
2011	The outbreak of the Syrian Civil War causes one of the biggest displacements of people since World War II
2012	President Obama signs the Deferred Action for Childhood Arrivals (DACA)
2014	German activists set up Refugees Welcome International, which arranges accommodation for refugees in private homes in 12 countries around the world
2017	US President Donald Trump orders the construction of a border wall along the whole of the US–Mexican border
2017	Some 740,000 Rohingya people are forced to flee from Myanmar to Bangladesh
2022	The Russian invasion of Ukraine causes the flight of some 6 million Ukrainian people to other countries; they are mostly women and children
2023	The *Adriana* fishing boat carrying over 750 migrants capsizes off the coast of Greece; only 104 people are rescued

Glossary

activist someone working to make change for the better

asylum seeker A person who seeks protection as a refugee under international law.

citizen Someone with legal rights and protection from a government

dawn raid unnannounced visit at dawn by police or other enforcement officers

deportation The act of forcing someone to leave a country

detention center A place, with strict conditions, where migrants are held

forced migration When people are forced to leave their homes due to threats such as conflict, violence, or persecution

homeland The country where a person was born

immigration The movement of people into a country

Indigenous native to a particular place

LGBTQ+ People who identify as lesbian, gay, bisexual, trans, queer, or other sexual and gender identities

migrant A person who leave their home country, usually because they want a better life

passport A document that proves the owner's identity and allows them to travel from country to country

people smuggler Someone who takes payment to arrange for people travel to another country illegally

refugee A person who migrates from their home country to escape persecution, war, and other kinds of violence and who seeks safety in another

visa A document issued by a country that gives permission for someone to go to that country and stay there for a set time

Further Information

Books

Backhaus, Jacklyn. *A New History of Immigration (True History).* Penguin Workshop, 2022

Goodman, Michael E. *The Refugee Crisis (Odysseys in Recent Events).* Creative Education, 2023

Krull, Kathleen. *American Immigration: Our History, Our Stories.* HarperCollins, 2020

Smith, Elliott. *Immigration, Refugees, and the Fight for a Better Life.* Lerner Publications, 2021

Websites

olympics.com/en/news/yusra-mardini-refugee-olympic-swimming-story
The remarkable story of Yusra Mardini, from saving lives to competing in the Olympics.

www.refugeesinternational.org/about-us/
Read about the work of Refugees International, which campaigns for the rights of refugees around the world.

www.statueofliberty.org/ellis-island/national-immigration-museum
Visit this site to find out about the migrants who passed through Ellis Island to make their home in the United States.

www.un.org/en/observances/migrants-day
More information about International Migrants Day and why it is held.

Index